THE FOOTPRINTS BOOK OF INSPIRATIONS

ALSO BY

MARGARET FISHBACK POWERS

Footprints: The True Story Behind the Poem That Inspired Millions

Friends of Footprints

The Footprints Book of Prayers

Footprints: A Heart for Children

Footprints Perpetual Calendar

Footprints: Scripture with Reflections Inspired by the Best-Loved Poem

Footprints: Images and Reflections of God's Presence

Margaret Fishback Powers

The Footprints Book of Inspirations

HarperCollins*PublishersLtd*

For information address
HarperCollins Publishers Ltd.,
55 Avenue Road, Suite 2900,
Toronto, Ontario, Canada M5R 3L2

www.harpercanada.com

HarperCollins books may be purchased for educational, business, or sales promotional use. For information please write: Special Markets Department, HarperCollins Canada,
55 Avenue Road, Suite 2900,
Toronto, Ontario, Canada M5R 3L2

This edition published 2002

Canadian Cataloguing in Publication Data

Powers, Margaret Fishback
The footprints book of inspirations

Previously published as Life's little inspiration book I, and II.
ISBN 0-00-200641-3

1. Christian life—Quotations, maxims, etc. I. Powers, Margaret Fishback. Life's little inspiration book. II. Title.

BV4832.3.P69 2002 242
C2002-900564-7

TC 9 8 7 6 5 4 3 2 1

Printed and bound in Canada
Set in Monotype Photina

Dedicated with loving memory and gratitude to Marguerite Elizabeth Watson for twenty years of constant support and encouragement. Marguerite was an unconditionally loving and accepting person, daily involving herself in many "mission activities," quietly in the background, yet always there to support me. God called her to His eternal reward in December 2001, in her eighty-second year.

FOREWORD

"As a man thinketh in his heart so is he." (Proverbs 23:7) This was one of my first collected gems as a child, and is still a favourite today.

The most difficult decision for a writer of "inspirational gems" is whether or not to select only her own personal favourites. I have tried to resist that temptation in this book by including many other gems of truth which have been uplifting in the lives of a number of my readers and personal friends.

I have endeavoured to select treasures that will help you recall memories of fulfilled promises and uplifting moments. It is my heart's desire that as you turn these pages of inspirational sayings, you too will discover a whisper of hope and comfort during moments of reflection that you never knew existed in this hectic world.

I trust these thoughts will encourage and stimulate you from day to day—like stepping stones as you follow in His Footprints on your journey of faith.

Continuing the Journey by Faith,
Margaret Fishback Powers
APRIL 2002

FOOTPRINTS

One night I dreamed a dream.
I was walking along the beach with my Lord.
Across the dark sky flashed scenes from my life.
For each scene, I noticed two sets
of footprints in the sand,
one belonging to me
and one to my Lord.
When the last scene of my life shot before me
I looked back at the footprints in the sand.
There was only one set of footprints.
I realized that this was at the lowest
and saddest times of my life.
This always bothered me
and I questioned the Lord
about my dilemma.
"Lord, you told me when I decided to follow You,
You would walk and talk with me all the way.
But I'm aware that during the most troublesome

times of my life there is only one set of footprints.
I just don't understand why, when I needed You most,
You leave me."
He whispered, "My precious child,
I love you and will never leave you
never, ever, during your trials and testings.
When you saw only one set of footprints
it was then that I carried you."

Written by
Margaret Fishback Powers,
THANKSGIVING, 1964

THE FOOTPRINTS BOOK OF INSPIRATIONS

Where the footprints of God lead you, the grace of God can keep you.

Blessed be the Lord, the God of Israel, who alone does wondrous things.

PSALM 72:18

The STOPS of a good man are ordered by the Lord as well as his STEPS.

(G. Mueller)

The Lord is good to those who wait for him . . .

LAMENTATIONS 3:25

Unless we reach our children's hearts today, they will break our hearts tomorrow.

(Paul L. Powers)

Suffer the little children to come unto me, and forbid them not: for of such is the kingdom of God.

MARK 10:14 AV

The caves of sorrow have mines of diamonds.

Weeping may linger for the night, but joy comes with the morning.

PSALM 30:5B

The world's largest mission field begins just outside your door.

. . . go and proclaim the kingdom of God.

LUKE 9:60B

Use your mistakes as a guidepost, not a hitching post.

If we confess our sins, he who is faithful and just will forgive us our sins and cleanse us from all unrighteousness.

I JOHN 1:9

Some people don't recognize opportunity because it comes dressed in work clothes.

In all toil there is profit, but mere talk leads only to poverty.

PROVERBS 14:23

'Do it NOW' is more than a motto: it's a way of life.

. . . See, now is the acceptable time; see, now is the day of salvation!

2 CORINTHIANS 6:2

Cheer up! The sun (Son) hasn't gone out of business.

Arise, shine; for thy light is come, and the glory of the Lord is risen upon thee.

ISAIAH 60:1 AV

Of all your worries, great or small, the worst of them never happened at all.

Do not worry about anything, but in everything by prayer and supplication with thanksgiving let your requests be made known to God.

PHILIPPIANS 4:6

Worry gives a small thing a big shadow.

And can any of you by worrying add a single hour to your span of life?

MATTHEW 6:27

Defeat isn't bitter if you don't swallow it.

Put away from you all bitterness and wrath and anger and wrangling and slander, together with all malice . . .

EPHESIANS 4:31

He who has a sharp tongue cuts his own throat.

From the same mouth come blessing and cursing. My brothers and sisters, this ought not to be so.

JAMES 3:10

If you learn from losing, then you haven't lost.

A rebuke strikes deeper into a discerning person than a hundred blows into a fool.

PROVERBS 17:10

The secret of spiritual advance is true and complete openness to God.

. . . him that cometh to me I will in no wise cast out.

JOHN 6:37 AV

The only safe and sure way to destroy enemies is to make them your friends.

But I say to you that listen, Love your enemies, do good to those who hate you . . .

LUKE 6:27

A selfish heart desires love for itself. A Christian heart delights to love—without return.

Whoever does not love does not know God, for God is love.

I JOHN 4:8

Some people drink at the fountain of knowledge; others just gargle.

. . . Let anyone who is thirsty come to me, and let the one who believes in me drink.

JOHN 7:37, 38

Forget your mistakes, but remember what they taught you.

And we know that all things work together for good to them that love God, to them who are called according to his purpose.

ROMANS 8:28 AV

Many little things are of greater value than big things. Could a cup of water exist without each drop?

. . . if you have faith the size of a mustard seed . . . nothing will be impossible for you.

MATTHEW 17:20

Experience is what is left over after you make a mistake.

When pride comes, then comes disgrace; but wisdom is with the humble.

PROVERBS 11:2

God formed us; sin deformed us; but Christ can transform us.

For all have sinned, and come short of the glory of God; being justified freely by his grace through the redemption that is in Christ Jesus.

ROMANS 3:23–24 AV

The God we worship writes His name on our faces.

. . . you will make me full of gladness with your presence.

ACTS 2:28B

Today, did you put your faith to test or to rest?

For I am not ashamed of the Gospel of Christ: for it is the power of God unto salvation to every one that believeth.

ROMANS 1:16A AV

You can't dream yourself into a character; you must forge yourself into one.

. . . suffering produces endurance, and endurance produces character, and character produces hope . . .

ROMANS 5:3B–4

As soon as the soul ceases to grow, the man is dead.

To set the mind on the flesh is death, but to set the mind on the Spirit is life and peace.

ROMANS 8:6

Faith always takes the first step forward.

Now the Lord said to Abram, 'Go from your country and your kindred . . . to the land that I will show you . . . '. So Abram went, as the Lord had told him.

GENESIS 12:1, 4A

Bitterness is like a boomerang: the moment you fling it, it returns.

A soft answer turns away wrath, but a harsh word stirs up anger.

PROVERBS 15:1

Never measure the mountain until you have reached the top; then you will see how low it is.

. . . the God who girded me with strength
. . . set me secure on the heights.

PSALM 18:32A, 33B

God has great confidence in you to place you where you are.

Here am I, the servant of the Lord; let it be with me according to your word.

LUKE 1:38

We stop forgiving others, when Christ stops forgiving us.

And if the same person sins against you seven times a day, and turns back to you seven times and says, 'I repent', you must forgive.

LUKE 17:4

You will never win the world with your spare cash.

Honour the Lord with your substance . . .
then your barns will be filled with plenty.

PROVERBS 3:9, 10

If we have pleasant thoughts, even when we are alone, we are in good company.

I remember the days of old, I think about all your deeds, I meditate on the works of your hands.

PSALM 143:5

Thought is the soul's chariot; a thoughtless man doesn't let his soul go anywhere.

You know when I sit down and when I rise up; you discern my thoughts from far away.
PSALM 139:2

The world is not a playground; it is a schoolroom.

So teach us to count our days that we may gain a wise heart.

PSALM 90:12

You can't break God's promises by leaning on them.

What then are we to say was gained by Abraham . . . ? No distrust made him waver concerning the promise of God, but he grew strong in his faith as he gave glory to God.

ROMANS 4:1, 20

If you find excuses for sin, your sin will never be excused.

For I acknowledge my transgressions: and my sin is ever before me.

PSALM 51:3 AV

Prepare and prevent instead of repair and repent.

Therefore you also must be ready, for the Son of Man is coming at an unexpected hour.

MATTHEW 24:44

More depends on will power than brain power.

Choose life . . . loving the Lord your God, obeying him, and holding fast to him; for that means life to you and length of days . . .

DEUTERONOMY 30:19B, 20A

They greatly dare who greatly trust.

So Daniel was taken up out of the den, and no kind of harm was found on him, because he had trusted in God.

DANIEL 6:23B

If our faith were greater, our deeds would be larger.

Whatever you ask for in prayer with faith, you will receive.

MATTHEW 21:22

I am responsible to God for the talent He has given me.

. . . to one he gave five talents, to another two, to another one, to each according to his ability. . .

MATTHEW 25:15

A man who goes through life looking for a soft thing can find it under his hat.

The appetite of the lazy craves, and gets nothing, while the appetite of the diligent is richly supplied.

PROVERBS 13:4

To take care of oneself is the first law of nature, but to deny oneself is the first law of grace.

If any want to become my followers, let them deny themselves and take up their cross and follow me.

MARK 8:34

Educate children without faith, and you make a race of clever devils.

(Duke of Wellington)

Train children in the right way, and when old, they will not stray.

PROVERBS 22:6

Think less about your rights and more about your duties.

Do not be deceived . . . for you reap whatever you sow.

GALATIANS 6:7

Conversion to Christ makes useful saints out of useless sinners.

So if anyone is in Christ, there is a new creation: everything old has passed away.

2 CORINTHIANS 5:17

The glory of God is a man fully alive.

(Irenaeus)

You see that faith was active along with [Abraham's] works, and faith was brought to completion by the works . . . and he was called the friend of God.

JAMES 2:22, 23

Trouble starts when we become our brother's keeper and cease to be his friend.

Let each of you look not to your own interests, but to the interests of others. Let the same mind be in you that was in Christ Jesus . . .

PHILIPPIANS 2:4–5

The final test of faith is not how much you believe, but how much you love.

You shall love the Lord your God with all your heart, and with all your soul, and with all your strength, and with all your mind.

LUKE 10:27

Wherever the Spirit of the Lord sways a heart, there is a passion to serve.

. . . let us consider how to provoke one another to love and good deeds.

HEBREWS 10:24

No smile is so beautiful as the one that struggles through tears.

He will yet fill your mouth with laughter, and your lips with shouts of joy.

JOB 8:21

With every rising of the sun, think of your life as just begun.

The steadfast love of the Lord never ceases, his mercies never come to an end; they are new every morning.

LAMENTATIONS 3:22–23

It is better to forgive and forget than to resent and remember.

. . . forgive us our debts, as we forgive our debtors.

MATTHEW 6:12 AV

The tongue, being in a wet place, slippeth.

(Paul L. Powers)

. . . the tongue is a small member, yet it boasts of great exploits. How great a forest is set ablaze by a small fire!

JAMES 3:5

As you think, so you are; you make or mar your success.

. . . whatsoever things are true, whatsoever things are honest, whatsoever things are just, whatsoever things are pure, whatsoever things are lovely, whatsoever things are of good report . . . think on these things.

PHILIPPIANS 4:8 AV

With the last step of the race you cross the finishing line.

. . . let him that thinketh he standeth take heed lest he fall.

I CORINTHIANS 10:12 AV

Being faithful on the job beats carrying a rabbit's foot for luck.

Many proclaim themselves loyal, but who can find one worthy of trust?

PROVERBS 20:6

The soul would have no rainbow if the eyes had no tears.

O that my head were a spring of water, and my eyes a fountain of tears. . .

JEREMIAH 9:1A

Great souls have wills; feeble ones, only wishes.

I am coming soon; hold fast to what you have, so that no one may seize your crown.

REVELATION 3:11

Count the day lost, when you have done no worthy deed.

What good is it, my brothers and sisters, if you say you have faith but do not have works?

JAMES 2:14

Call on God for help, but row away from the rocks.

When the righteous cry for help, the Lord hears, and rescues them from all their troubles.

PSALM 34:17

Some tread lightly through life; others crush the flowers.

Let your gentleness be known to everyone.

PHILIPPIANS 4:5

Children are likely to see God as Father, if they see God in their father.

. . . the glory of children is their parents.

PROVERBS 17:6B

No work in the world pays like mother's work.

Then he went down with them and came to Nazareth, and was obedient to them. His mother treasured all these things in her heart.

LUKE 2:51

God sees tomorrow more clearly than we see yesterday.

He calls his own sheep by name . . . he goes ahead of them, and the sheep follow him because they know his voice.

JOHN 10:3, 4

A true friend is like the shade of a great tree in the noonday heat.

A friend loves at all times, and kinsfolk are born to share adversity.

PROVERBS 17:17

It's easier to pick a wise man by the things he doesn't say.

One who spares words is knowledgeable.

PROVERBS 17:27A

The lazier we are today, the more we have to do tomorrow.

The way of the lazy is overgrown with thorns.

PROVERBS 15:19A

The truest expression of Christianity is not a sigh, but a song.

Let the word of Christ dwell in you richly . . . and with gratitude in your hearts sing psalms, hymns, and spiritual songs to God.

COLOSSIANS 3:16

The beginning is half of the whole.

. . . the one who began a good work among you will bring it to completion by the day of Jesus Christ.

PHILIPPIANS 1:6

When life writes 'Ended,' the angels write 'Begun.'

Those who believe in me, even though they die, will live.

JOHN 11:25B

Songs are heartbursts of gladness.

For this I will extol you, O Lord, among the nations, and sing praises to your name.

2 SAMUEL 22:50

Love is like a bank: the more you put in, the more your interest grows.

For I have given you an example, that ye should do as I have done to you.

JOHN 13:15 AV

There can be no rainbow unless it has rained.

. . . your Father . . . makes his sun rise on the evil and on the good, and sends rain on the righteous and on the unrighteous.

MATTHEW 5:45

The first duty of every Christian is to be sure he lays no stumbling block in another's way.

If any of you put a stumbling block before one of these little ones who believe in me, it would be better for you if a great millstone were hung around your neck and you were thrown into the sea.

MARK 9:42

Some folk are born fools, but the majority of us become so through practice.

The mouths of fools are their ruin, and their lips a snare to themselves.

PROVERBS 18:7

Calvary restored mankind's lost inheritance.

God so loved the world, that he gave his only begotten Son, that whosoever believeth in him should not perish, but have everlasting life.

JOHN 3:16 AV

The main reason our Lord gives for not worrying about the future is that it's completely in His hands.

Do not let your hearts be troubled . . . In my Father's house there are many dwelling places. If it were not so, would I have told you that I go to prepare a place for you?

JOHN 14:1A, 2

The best way to live in the world is to live above it.

If any man love the world, the love of the Father is not in him.

I JOHN 2:15 AV

Your church may point you to Heaven,
but it cannot carry you there.

Who shall ascend into the hill of the Lord? Or who shall stand in his holy place? He that hath clean hands, and a pure heart . . .

PSALM 24:3–4A AV

Failure's other names: wait, tomorrow, too busy, good enough, not my job.

Instead, put on the Lord Jesus Christ, and make no provision for the flesh, to gratify its desires.

ROMANS 13:14

A man knows the least of the influence of his own life.

. . . whoever wishes to become great among you must be your servant.

MARK 10:43

Misunderstanding is the source of untold sorrows.

. . . they are to avoid wrangling over words, which does no good but only ruins those who are listening.

2 TIMOTHY 2:14

Serving Christ under law is a duty, under love is a delight.

For the love of Christ urges us on.

2 CORINTHIANS 5:14

One life can influence an entire community, just as a flower can fill a room with sweet perfume.

Those who are wise shall shine like the brightness of the sky, and those who lead many to righteousness, like the stars for ever and ever.

DANIEL 12:3

A man may buy a house, but only a woman can make it a home.

A capable wife . . . looks well to the ways of her household.

PROVERBS 31:10A, 27A

When the OUTLOOK is not good, try the UPLOOK.

But filled with the Holy Spirit, [Stephen] gazed into heaven and saw the glory of God and Jesus standing at the right hand of God.

ACTS 7:55

So-called innocent amusements of the world are only contrivances to forget God.

When you have eaten your fill, take care that you do not forget the Lord.

DEUTERONOMY 6:11B–12A

Of all the things you wear, your expression is the most important.

. . . you make him glad with the joy of your presence.

PSALM 21:6B

Success lies not in what we start, but in what we finish.

And let us not be weary in well doing: for in due season we shall reap, if we faint not.

GALATIANS 6:9 AV

Faith is the vision of the heart. It sees God in the dark, as in the day.

The just shall live by faith.

ROMANS 1:17B AV

Aim to carve your name on hearts, not on marble.

Come and hear, all ye that fear God, and I will declare what he hath done for my soul.

PSALM 66:16 AV

Before you tell someone your troubles, ask yourself, would I listen to theirs?

If one gives answer before hearing, it is folly and shame.

PROVERBS 18:13

Those who are drawn towards Christ are necessarily drawn towards each other.

. . . but if we walk in the light as he himself is in the light, we have fellowship with one another . . .

I JOHN 1:7

God gives us crosses in this life, so that we may wear crowns in the next.

To him that overcometh will I grant to sit with me in my throne, even as I also overcame, and am set down with my Father in his throne.

REVELATION 3:21 AV

Grudges, like babies, grow larger when nursed.

Beloved, do not grumble against one another.

JAMES 5:9A

What you leave IN your children should be more than what you leave TO them.

Sons are indeed a heritage from the Lord, the fruit of the womb a reward.

PSALM 127:3

To have an upright life, lean on Jesus.

. . . whoso putteth his trust in the Lord shall be safe.

PROVERBS 29:25B AV

Repentant prayer is one weapon Satan cannot duplicate.

I tell you, there is joy in the presence of the angels of God over one sinner who repents.

LUKE 15:10

The crowns we cast at Jesus' feet must all be won on earth.

For this slight momentary affliction is preparing us for an eternal weight of glory beyond all measure . . .

2 CORINTHIANS 4:17

When we open our hearts to Jesus, God opens our minds to His Word.

Those who are unspiritual do not receive the gifts of God's Spirit, for they are foolishness to them, and they are unable to understand them because they are spiritually discerned.

I CORINTHIANS 2:14

There is but one easy place in this world,
that is the grave.

(Beecher)

Therefore, my beloved, be steadfast, immovable, always excelling in the work of the Lord, because you know that in the Lord your labour is not in vain.

I CORINTHIANS 15:58

Work that is cheerfully done is usually well done.

And whatsoever ye do, do it heartily, as to the Lord, and not unto men . . . for ye serve the Lord Christ.

COLOSSIANS 3:23–24 AV

The best way to kill time is to work it to death.

God blessed the seventh day and hallowed it, because on it God rested from all the work that he had done in creation.

GENESIS 2:3

The easiest way to keep temptation from growing is to nip it in the bud.

Keep awake and pray that you may not come into the time of trial; the spirit indeed is willing, but the flesh is weak.

MARK 14:38

Great faithfulness is exhibited not so much in ability to do, as to suffer.

Do not fear what you are about to suffer . . . Be faithful until death, and I will give you the crown of life.

REVELATION 2:10

It is good to follow in the footsteps of a pastor who follows in the footprints of the Master.

Our steps are made firm by the Lord, when he delights in our way.

PSALM 37:23

When tempted to lose patience with someone, stop and think how patient God has been with you.

Love is patient; love is kind.

I CORINTHIANS 13:4A

Great results cannot be achieved at once, but as we walk—step by step.

. . . the Lord direct your hearts into the love of God, and into the patient waiting for Christ.

2 THESSALONIANS 3:5 AV

Every footstep in life trembles with possibilities; every mile is big with destiny.

My steps have held fast to your paths; my feet have not slipped.

PSALM 17:5

The one base thing in the universe is to receive favours and render none.

For where there is envy and selfish ambition, there will also be disorder . . . But the wisdom from above is first pure, then peaceable, gentle, willing to yield, full of mercy and good fruits, without a trace of partiality or hypocrisy.

JAMES 3:16–17

Life is a succession of lessons, which must be lived to be understood.

Blessed are those who hunger and thirst for righteousness, for they will be filled.

MATTHEW 5:6

We gain strength from temptations we resist.

Resist the devil, and he will flee from you.

JAMES 4:7 AV

There is no trait of character more enriching than simple humility.

For all who exalt themselves will be humbled, and those who humble themselves will be exalted.

LUKE 14:11

The most important thing is not so much where we stand as the direction in which we are going.

Be strong and bold; have no fear or dread . . . because it is the Lord your God who goes with you.

DEUTERONOMY 31:6

To win takes not luck but pluck; not
wishbone but backbone.

By your endurance you will gain your souls.

LUKE 21:19

A man is tomorrow what he thinks today.

Set your affection on things above, not on things on the earth.

COLOSSIANS 3:2 AV

Darkness cannot put out the Light; it can only make Him brighter.

The light shines in the darkness, and the darkness did not overcome it.

JOHN 1:5

God made our faces round; only we can make them long.

And whenever you fast, do not look dismal, like the hypocrites, for they disfigure their faces so as to show others that they are fasting. Truly I tell you, they have received their reward.

MATTHEW 6:16

As we grow older, we acquire the faces we deserve.

A glad heart makes a cheerful countenance.

PROVERBS 15:13

Judging from church attendance, there won't be many men in heaven.

If we say that we have fellowship with him, and walk in darkness, we lie, and do not live by the truth.

I JOHN 1:6 AV

Few people get dizzy from doing too many good turns.

As God's chosen ones, holy and beloved, clothe yourselves with compassion, kindness, humility, meekness, and patience.

COLOSSIANS 3:12

A sure way to freeze to death is to be wrapped up in yourself.

A person's pride will bring humiliation, but one who is lowly in spirit will obtain honour.

PROVERBS 29:23

The only way some people get exercise is by throwing bouquets at themselves.

. . . ungodly sinners . . . are bombastic in speech, flattering people to their own advantage.

JUDE 1:15, 16

There are two difficult things in life: one is to make a name for yourself, the other is to keep it.

A good name is to be chosen rather than great riches, and favour is better than silver or gold.

PROVERBS 22:1

Each one of us should keep a large cemetery to bury the faults of our friends.

Above all, maintain constant love for one another, for love covers a multitude of sins.

I PETER 4:8

Others will follow your footsteps more easily than they will follow your advice.

As Jesus was walking along, he saw a man called Matthew sitting at the tax booth; and he said to him, 'Follow me'. And he got up and followed him.

MATTHEW 9:9

When the heart is converted, the wallet will be inverted.

. . . the righteous give and do not hold back.

PROVERBS 21:26

Don't give from the top of the purse, but from the bottom of the heart.

For all of them have contributed out of their abundance, but she out of her poverty has put in all she had to live on.

LUKE 21:4

God demands a whole heart, but cradles a broken one.

He heals the brokenhearted, and binds up their wounds.

PSALM 147:3

Being bald has its advantages. When company comes all you have to straighten is your tie.

. . . the very hairs of your head are all numbered.

MATTHEW 10:30 AV

Enthusiasm is the greatest business asset in the world.

Do not lag in zeal, be ardent in spirit, serve the Lord.

ROMANS 12:11

Clouds may cover the sunshine, but they cannot banish the sun.

The sun shall be no more thy light by day . . . but the Lord shall be unto thee an everlasting light.

ISAIAH 60:19 AV

Courage is the anchor that holds one steady, and enables one to climb on and on.

Be of good courage, and he shall strengthen your heart, all ye that hope in the Lord.

PSALM 31:24 AV

Becoming a Christian is letting the love of God into your heart and soul.

Listen! I am standing at the door, knocking; if you hear my voice and open the door, I will come in to you and eat with you and you with me.

REVELATION 3:20

A friend is the first person to come in when others go out.

. . . a true friend sticks closer than one's nearest kin.

PROVERBS 18:24B

Through the footprints of faith we see in Jesus everything that God IS.

No one has ever seen God. It is God the only Son . . . who has made him known.

JOHN 1:18

God will only carry those who allow Him to carry them.

I the Lord have called thee in righteousness, and will hold thine hand, and will keep thee . . .

ISAIAH 42:6

Faith unlocks the door to ultimate achievement.

. . . Keep alert, stand firm in your faith, be courageous, be strong.

I CORINTHIANS 16:13

He who harbors a grudge will miss the haven of happiness.

But I say to you that if you are angry with a brother or a sister, you will be liable to judgment . . .

MATTHEW 5:22

Man's littleness is expressed by the presence of the stars.

See the highest stars, how lofty they are!

JOB 22:12

Happiness is where it is found, but seldom where it is sought.

(J. Billings)

I turned my mind to know and to search out and to see wisdom . . .

ECCLESIASTES 7:25

Defeat may serve as well as victory to shake the soul and let the glory out.

. . . thanks be to God, who gives us the victory through our Lord Jesus Christ.

I CORINTHIANS 15:57

Even though you do the right thing, do you do it in the right way?

In all your ways acknowledge him, and he will make straight your paths.

PROVERBS 3:6

Our greatest glory is not in never falling, but in rising every time we fall.

Humble yourselves before the Lord, and he will exalt you.

JAMES 4:10

If you love your friends, learn when to leave them.

The heart of the wise teacheth his mouth, and addeth learning to his lips.

PROVERBS 16:23

Learning how to bear inescapable sorrow is not easily done.

. . . have unity of spirit, sympathy, love for one another, a tender heart, and a humble mind.

I PETER 3:8

In the matter of salvation, he who hesitates is lost!

. . . God proves his love for us in that while we still were sinners Christ died for us.

ROMANS 5:8

God's treasure house, the Bible, is only unlocked by the golden key of meditation.

This book . . . thou shalt meditate therein day and night . . .

JOSHUA 1:8

Nature is an outstretched finger pointing towards God!

O Lord, how manifold are your works!

PSALM 104:24

When Christ prepares the table for us it is always a well-balanced meal.

(H. K. Barclay)

You prepare a table before me in the presence of my enemies . . . my cup overflows.

PSALM 23:5

Salvation is free, but you have to ask for it.
(Paul L. Powers)

Ask, and it will be given you; search, and you will find . . .

LUKE 11:9

Without encouragement, any one of us can lose confidence.

. . . the fruit of the Spirit is love, joy, peace, patience, kindness, generosity . . .

GALATIANS 5:22

Before becoming an effective worker for the Lord, take time to study The Manual.

I treasure your word in my heart, so that I may not sin against you.

PSALM 119:11

Home—a place where the small are great, and the great are small.

Seek ye first the kingdom of God, and his righteousness; and all these things shall be added unto you.

MATTHEW 6:33

The name of Jesus may be a byword to the sinner, but it is a password to Heaven for the saint.

". . . the Messiah . . . Whose son is he?" They said to him, "The son of David."

MATTHEW 22:42

You cannot whitewash yourself by blackening others.

. . . and be kind to one another . . . forgiving one another, as God in Christ has forgiven you.

EPHESIANS 4:32

I can't see the pattern into which each tangled thread is bent, but in trusting the Father, I am content.

. . . for I have learned to be content with whatever I have.

PHILIPPIANS 4:11

In the Christian life, an ounce of truth is worth a ton of talk.

Let the wise also hear and gain in learning . . .

PROVERBS 1:5

A happy memory is the most valuable thing in the world. It's a hiding place for "unforgotten treasures."

(Paul L. Powers)

Take delight in the Lord, and he will give you the desires of your heart.

PSALM 37:4

Sooner or later, all of us come to a "Red Sea" place in life.

The Lord drove the sea back . . . and turned it into dry land . . . The Israelites went into the sea on dry ground.

EXODUS 14:21–22

Don’t just count your years, make your years count!

(Dr Ernest Meyers)

I know that there is nothing better for them than to be happy and enjoy themselves as long as they live . . .

ECCLESIASTES 3:12

An optimist is someone who thinks the future is uncertain.

Teach me the way I should go, for to you I lift up my soul.

PSALM 143:8

The Lord seeks men and women who are not ashamed to be seen down on their knees in prayer.

Then he withdrew from them about a stone's throw, knelt down, and prayed . . .

LUKE 22:41

God is more concerned about your response to the problem than He is in removing the problem.

My eyes are ever toward the Lord, for he will pluck my feet out of the net.

PSALM 25:15

It's a wise parent who knows how to encourage a child's hidden talent.

. . . do not provoke your children to anger, but bring them up in the discipline and instruction of the Lord.

EPHESIANS 6:4

The answer always comes, but often as not in ways you least expect.

Call to me and I will answer you, and will tell you great and hidden things that you have not known.

JEREMIAH 33:3

LIFE—Warning: hazardous journey ahead. Be prepared for detours.

(Paul L. Powers)

Do not enter the path of the wicked, and do not walk in the path of evildoers.

PROVERBS 4:14

Other books were given for information;
the Bible was given for transformation.

. . . be transformed by the renewing of your minds, so that you may discern what is the will of God . . .

ROMANS 12:2

The most overloaded, desperate people are those who can see no other burdens but their own.

Bear one another's burdens, and in this way you will fulfill the law of Christ.

GALATIANS 6:2

The character you end life with will be the character you begin eternity with.

For God hath not appointed us to wrath, but to obtain salvation by our Lord Jesus Christ.

I THESSALONIANS 5:9

The whole secret of prolonging one's life consists in doing nothing to shorten it.

For once you were darkness, but now in the Lord you are light. Live as children of light . . .

EPHESIANS 5:8

A best friend is someone who is in your corner when you are cornered.

. . . a true friend sticks closer than one's nearest kin.

PROVERBS 18:24

Temptation is something you can't use at a price you can't resist.

And lead us not into temptation, but deliver us from evil.

MATTHEW 6:13

A mistake a lot of preachers make is to think that they've been anointed, not appointed.

For this gospel I was appointed a herald and an apostle and a teacher.

2 TIMOTHY 1:11

Confidence is the feeling that you have before you really understand the problem.

The wise are cautious and turn away from evil, but the fool throws off restraint and is careless.

PROVERBS 14:16

The reason many people don't live within their income is because they don't consider that living.

For what will it profit them to gain the whole world and forfeit their life?

MARK 8:36

God allows us to be in darkness so He can show us He is the Light.

The people who walked in darkness have seen a great light . . .

ISAIAH 9:2B

If you want the world to take notice of you, don't sell yourself short.

The laborer is worthy of his reward.

I TIMOTHY 5:18

The only thing worse than growing old is being denied the privilege.

Do not cast me off in the time of old age; do not forsake me when my strength is spent.

PSALM 71:9

If poverty is a blessing in disguise, then in many cases the disguise is perfect.

. . . give me neither poverty nor riches; feed me with the food that I need.

PROVERBS 30:8

Life with Christ is an endless hope; without Him, a hopeless end.

. . . God chose to make known how great . . . are the riches of the glory of this mystery, which is Christ in you, the hope of glory.

COLOSSIANS 1:27

People are lonely because they build walls instead of bridges.

Do not be far from me, for trouble is near and there is no one to help.

PSALM 22:11

Man builds for a century; the Christian builds for eternity.

. . . this one thing I do: forgetting what lies behind and straining forward to what lies ahead.

PHILIPPIANS 3:13

Christ helps us to face the music, even when we don't like the tune.

What time I am afraid, I will trust in thee.

PSALM 56:3

Kindness has converted more sinners than zeal, eloquence or learning.

"How beautiful are the feet of those who bring good news!"

ROMANS 10:15

Lost time is never found again!
(Paul L. Powers)

For everything there is a season, and a time for every matter under heaven . . .
ECCLESIASTES 3:1

The first step to victory: recognize the enemy!

(Paul L. Powers)

Put on the whole armour of God, so that you may be able to stand against the wiles of the devil.

EPHESIANS 6:11

Well done is better than well said.

Ye are my friends, if ye do whatsoever I command you.

JOHN 15:14

Where God guides, He provides!

". . . you will have treasure in heaven; then come, follow me."

MARK 10:21

Is your life a witness, with testimony true? Could the world be won to Christ by what others see in you?

(Paul L. Powers)

. . . let your light shine before others, so that they may see your good works and give glory to your Father in heaven.

MATTHEW 5:16

Instead of counting your troubles, try adding up your blessings!

(Dr Geoffrey Still)

. . . who has blessed us in Christ with every spiritual blessing in the heavenly places . . .

EPHESIANS 1:3

Trials should make us better—not bitter.

And whosoever doth not bear his cross, and come after me, cannot be my disciple.

LUKE 14:27

Blessed is the soul who is too busy to worry during the day and too tired to worry at night.

Be still before the Lord, and wait patiently for him . . .

PSALM 37:7

Child's prayer overheard at camp: "Dear Jesus, I'll come again, 'cause I like myself when I'm near you."

(Paul L. Powers)

Whosoever therefore shall humble himself as this little child, the same is greatest in the kingdom of Heaven.

MATTHEW 18:4

Christ is well known for working three days ahead of schedule.

(Paula Powers)

"I will destroy this temple . . . and in three days I will build another . . ."

MARK 14:58

A smooth sea never made a skillful sailor.

. . . be instant in season, out of season; reprove, rebuke, exhort with all longsuffering and doctrine.

2 TIMOTHY 4:2

God is too good to be unkind and too wise to make mistakes.

O Lord, you have searched me and known me . . . and are acquainted with all my ways.

PSALM 139:1, 3

Pray believing, have faith and then trust!
(Dr Ernest Meyers)

Trust in the Lord with all your heart . . .
In all your ways acknowledge Him . . .
PROVERBS 3:5, 6

Disappointment and sorrow come to all. There is no new individual experience in life—only parallel cases.

For we ourselves were once foolish . . . But when the goodness and loving kindness of God our Saviour appeared, he saved us . . .

TITUS 3:3–5

You can only be ready to live if you are ready to die.

(John & Betty Stamm, martyred missionaries)

Yes, we do have confidence, and we would rather be away from the body and at home with the Lord.

2 CORINTHIANS 5:8

In creation we see God's hand; in redemption we see His heart.

. . . Christ Jesus . . . gave himself to redeem all mankind.

I TIMOTHY 2:6

God's grace: EVERYTHING for NOTHING, when we don't deserve ANYTHING.

. . . the Lord will give grace and glory: no good thing will he withhold from them that walk uprightly.

PSALM 84:11

Your greatest gift to others is a good example.

(Dr Geoffrey Still)

... Christ also suffered for you, leaving you an example, so that you should follow in his steps.

I PETER 2:21

Man needs more than a new start, he needs a new heart.

I the Lord test the mind and search the heart . . .

JEREMIAH 17:10

When walking through the "valley of shadows," remember, a shadow is cast by a Light.

(H. K. Barclay)

Even though I walk through the darkest valley, I fear no evil . . .

PSALM 23:4

There is always an “I” in the middle of sIn.

(Paul L. Powers)

How many are my iniquities and my sins?

JOB 13:23

The problem with doing nothing is you can't stop to take a rest.

"Come away to a deserted place all by yourselves and rest a while."

MARK 6:31

When you meet temptation, keep to the right!

Pray that ye enter not into temptation.

LUKE 22:40

Today's seed brings tomorrow's harvest.

May those who sow in tears reap with shouts of joy.

PSALM 126:5

Never borrow sorrow from tomorrow.

Banish anxiety from your mind, and put away pain from your body . . .

ECCLESIASTES 11:10

Narrow minds and wide mouths bring trouble!

(Paul L. Powers)

". . . let them keep their tongues from evil and their lips from speaking deceit . . ."

I PETER 3:10

Prayer cuts knots you can't untie!

May the Lord fulfill all your petitions.

PSALM 20:5

Would people rather see you coming or going?

. . . God will make you worthy of his call and will fulfill by his power every good resolve and work of faith . . .

2 THESSALONIANS 1:11

You can't break God's promises by leaning on them!

Cast all your anxieties on him, because he cares for you.

I PETER 5:7

If you plant weeds, don't expect to grow flowers!

The wicked worketh a deceitful work: but to him that soweth righteousness shall be a sure reward.

PROVERBS 11:18

God very often digs wells of joy with the spade of sorrow.

The Lord is close to the brokenhearted and saves those who are crushed in spirit.

PSALM 34:18

Tell EVERYONE about the ONLY ONE who can save ANYONE!

"I am the way, and the truth, and the life. No one comes to the Father except through me."

JOHN 14:6

Patience carries a lot of WAIT!

. . . so that you may not become sluggish, but imitators of those who through faith and patience inherit the promises.

HEBREWS 6:12

When it comes to prayer some people need a FAITH lift.

(Paula Powers)

. . . let us work for the good of all, and especially for those of the family of faith.

GALATIANS 6:10

The fruit of the Christian is ripened in Sonshine!

But grow in the grace and knowledge of our Lord and Saviour Jesus Christ.

2 PETER 3:18

Prayer does not need proof, it needs practice.

What things soever ye desire, when ye pray, believe that ye receive them, and ye shall have them.

MARK 11:24

Angry at another's faults? Count ten—of your own!

One who is slow to anger is better than the mighty . . .

PROVERBS 16:32

Christ has a message for this MESS AGE.

(Dr Barry Moore)

At that day ye shall know that I am in my Father, and ye in me, and I in you.

JOHN 14:20

Treasures in Heaven are laid up only as treasures on earth are laid down.

For where your treasure is, there your heart will be also.

MATTHEW 6:21

Is your memory rusty because your Bible is dusty?

With my whole heart I seek you; do not let me stray from your commandments.

PSALM 119:10

The Bible is the only book whose author is always present when it is read.

"I am the Alpha and the Omega," says the Lord God, who is and who was and who is to come, the Almighty.

REVELATION 1:8

You never get a second chance to make a first impression.

Let your speech be always with grace, seasoned with salt . . .

COLOSSIANS 4:6

The poorest man is he whose only wealth is money.

(Dr Leroy Gager)

Keep your lives free from the love of money, and be content with what you have . . .

HEBREWS 13:5

God has included you in His plans—have you included Him in yours?

(Paul L. Powers)

For surely I know the plans I have for you, says the Lord, plans for your welfare and not for harm . . .

JEREMIAH 29:11

After all is said and done, more is usually said than done!

For God will bring every deed into judgment, including every secret thing, whether good or evil.

ECCLESIASTES 12:14

Easy street is a blind alley.

There is a way that seems right to a person,
but its end is the way to death.

PROVERBS 14:12

Each cross, each trouble has its day—
then passes away.

. . . but they that seek the Lord shall not want any good thing.

PSALM 34:10

Praise does wonders for the sense of hearing.

But exhort one another daily . . . lest any of you be hardened through the deceitfulness of sin.

HEBREWS 3:13

A clear conscience is often the sign of a bad memory.

Depart from evil, and do good; seek peace, and pursue it.

PSALM 34:14

Surrounded by peace, no one is ever alone.

Keep on doing the things that you have learned . . . and seen in me, and the God of peace will be with you.

PHILIPPIANS 4:9

You don't stop laughing because you grow old—you grow old because you stop laughing.

A cheerful heart is a good medicine . . .

PROVERBS 17:22

A Godly home: a father's kingdom, a mother's world, a child's paradise.

I came that they may have life, and have it abundantly.

JOHN 10:10

Beware of hypocrisy—it is better to be one-sided than two-faced!

So you also on the outside look righteous to others, but inside you are full of hypocrisy and lawlessness.

MATTHEW 23:28

Keep your light shining. God will put it where it can be seen.

While you have the light, believe in the light, so that you may become children of light.

JOHN 12:36

SCARS for Christ today mean STARS for Christ tomorrow!

From now on, let no one make trouble for me; for I carry the marks of Jesus branded on my body.

GALATIANS 6:17

Man measures his deed; God measures the intentions.

That ye might walk worthy of the Lord unto all pleasing, being fruitful in every good work . . .

COLOSSIANS 1:10

Witnessing for Christ is not getting into the MOOD but being in the MODE.

(Paula Powers)

"Whom shall I send, and who will go for us?" And I said "Here am I; send me!"

ISAIAH 6:8

We learn from experience. A man never wakes his second baby just to see her smile.

"I have acquired great wisdom . . . my mind has had great experience of wisdom and knowledge."

ECCLESIASTES 1:16

The best bridge between despair and hope is a good night's sleep.

He shall enter into peace: they shall rest in their beds, each one walking in his uprightness.

ISAIAH 57:2

Keep your confidence in God and He'll keep your cares.

(H. K. Barclay)

. . . for the Lord will be your confidence and will keep your foot from being caught.

PROVERBS 3:26

No service is fruitful, unless done in the power of the Holy Spirit.

If we live in the Spirit, let us also walk in the Spirit.

GALATIANS 5:25

All God's testings have a purpose; someday you will see the light.

But for now just put your trust in Him; walk by faith, not by sight. How lovely is your dwelling place, O Lord of hosts!

PSALM 84:1

Don't be so concerned about working for God that you overlook dwelling with God.

I pray that . . . Christ may dwell in your hearts through faith, as you are being rooted and grounded in love.

EPHESIANS 3:16, 17

A good Christian shows the way, knows the way and goes the way.

He will feed his flock like a shepherd; he will gather the lambs in his arms . . . and gently lead the mother sheep.

ISAIAH 40:11

Remember that the sign on the door to opportunity reads: PUSH.

. . . that God would open unto us a door of utterance, to speak the mystery of Christ . . .

COLOSSIANS 4:3

In going out into the world, we often carry our "grief case" to do the daily work of the Lord.

Rejoice with those who rejoice, weep with those who weep.

ROMANS 12:15

The age of understanding and acceptance comes to different people at different times.

Come now, and let us reason together, saith the Lord . . .

ISAIAH 1:18

The powers of the soul are commensurate with its needs.

. . . what does the Lord require of you but to do justice, and to love kindness . . .

MICAH 6:8

The Resurrection makes a difference—
the difference between life and death,
light and darkness, hope and despair.

By his great mercy he has given us a new birth into a living hope through the resurrection of Jesus Christ from the dead . . .

I PETER 1:3

Don't let your fears about the next hundred years discourage you from smiling now—occasionally, anyhow.

. . . fear not, for I am with thee, and will bless thee . . .

GENESIS 26:24

Once formed, the habit of prayer
becomes as natural as breathing.

Then Jesus told them a parable about their need to pray always and not to lose heart.

LUKE 18:1

No enemy is so near that God is not nearer.

. . . in the shadows of your wings I will take refuge, until the destroying storms pass by.

PSALM 57:1

Trust God to overcome your difficulties—he has had many thousands of years' experience.

Jesus Christ is the same yesterday and today and forever.

HEBREWS 13:8

Turn to God for help in shaping your life—by prayer he will bring peace to the humblest.

Just like the clay in the potter's hand, so are you in my hand, O house of Israel.

JEREMIAH 18:6

Bored people are not the under-
privileged but the over-privileged.

See the one who would not take refuge in God, but trusted in abundant riches, and sought refuge in wealth.

PSALM 52:7

Success in dealing with others is like making rhubarb pie—use all the sweetener you can, then double it!

Neither shall you bear false witness against your neighbour.

DEUTERONOMY 5:20

Prayer is: **T**hank-, **A**sk-, **L**isten-, **K**nowing—to God!

"You are my God; give ear, O Lord, to the voice of my supplications."

PSALM 140:6

Faith is continuing to run, confident that you will get your "second wind."

Brothers and sisters, do not be weary in doing what is right.

2 THESSALONIANS 3:13

Sometimes we don't read the writing on the wall because we can't see it properly.

Now my eyes will be open and my ears attentive to the prayer that is made in this place.

2 CHRONICLES 7:15

A kick in the pants sends you further along in life than a friendly handshake.

All scripture is inspired by God and is useful for teaching, for reproof, for correction, and for training in righteousness . . .

2 TIMOTHY 3:16

An honest salesperson is one who sells goods that don't come back, to customers who do.

. . . we are sure that we have a clear conscience, desiring to act honourably in all things.

HEBREWS 13:18

A modern woman is one who puts off today what her husband can do on the weekend.

The heart of her husband trusts in her, and he will have no lack of gain.

PROVERBS 31:11

A true missionary is God's child in God's place, doing God's work in God's way—for God's glory!

. . . because we look not at what can be seen but at what cannot be seen; for what can be seen is temporary, but what cannot be seen is eternal.

2 CORINTHIANS 4:18

When church services are over, your service begins.

And every day in the temple and at home they did not cease to teach and proclaim Jesus as the Messiah.

ACTS 5:42

Put God first—be happy at last!

"My heart exults in the Lord; my strength is exalted in my God."

I SAMUEL 2:1

Does your walk live up to your talk?
(B. Harback)

. . . though we stumble, we shall not fall headlong, for the Lord holds us by the hand.
PSALM 37:24

Most of us won't be content with our lot in life until it's a lot more.

Of course, there is great gain in godliness combined with contentment . . .

I TIMOTHY 6:6

Faith can never overdraw its account in the bank of Heaven.

"Whoever is faithful in a very little is faithful also in much . . ."

LUKE 16:10

Jesus Christ—the light that knows no power failure

(Paul L. Powers)

"I am the light of the world. Whoever follows me will never walk in darkness but will have the light of life."

JOHN 8:12